THE
DEATH
OF THE
HAT

A Brief History of Poetry
in 50 Objects

Selected by
Paul B. Janeczko

illustrated by
Chris Raschka

Candlewick Press

for my father

C. R.

Compilation copyright © 2015 by Paul B. Janeczko. Illustrations copyright © 2015 by Chris Raschka. Copyright acknowledgments appear on pages 76–77. All rights reserved. No part of this book may be reproduced, transmitted, or stored in an information retrieval system in any form or by any means, graphic, electronic, or mechanical, including photocopying, taping, and recording, without prior written permission from the publisher. First edition 2015. Library of Congress Catalog Card Number 2013957308. ISBN 978-0-7636-6963-8. This book was typeset in Myriad. The illustrations were done in watercolor and ink. Candlewick Press, 99 Dover Street, Somerville, Massachusetts 02144. visit us at www.candlewick.com. Printed in Shenzhen, Guangdong, China. 16 17 18 19 CCP 10 9 8 7 6 5 4 3

50 THANKS

None of my 50 books is the work of a single person.
Nor is my life or career the work of one person. I have been
blessed to have known many supportive and helpful people. It is
time to thank them.

I cannot imagine my career without my editorial/book family: Richard Jackson,
Liz Bicknell, M. Jerry Weiss, Lee Bennett Hopkins, Chris Raschka, Melissa Sweet, Hilary
Van Dusen, Wendy Murray, Barbara Kouts, and Tobey Antao.

My home family: Nadine Edris, who's been with me for all but half a dozen of the books, and
Emma Janeczko, who arrived on the scene after book 12.

My birth family: Mom, Dad, Jay, John, Mark, and Mary.

My extended family, including: Dick and Margaret Abrahamson; Susan and Scott
Bean; Terry and Cheryl Bowers; Connie Burns; Eileen Fair; Roger Frank; John,
Lori, and Aoife Gunn; Thom Hoffman and Louise Hamilton; Georgia Heard;
Kara LaReau; J. Patrick Lewis; Melanie May; Richard and Mary Lou Moore;
Jim Pierce; Lynn Plourde; Bob and Catherine Skapura; Norma Vogel;
Peter and Pam Vose; and Judy Mayne Wallis.

The merry band at Candlewick Press, especially Anne Irza-
Leggat, who answer questions and keep me from getting
lost at conferences and make me look better in
numerous ways.

And the other old guys at the diner:
Peter Berry, Tom Collins, and Chuck
Primozich.

P. B. J.

Contents

car

Modern Period » **1900–1945**

rooster cup

Postmodern Period » **1945–present**

cruise ship

Contemporary

viola

starfish

Introduction

Each anthology I create presents its own challenges. Finding poems is often the easy part. I have more than 1,500 poetry books and four file cabinet drawers stuffed with individual poems.

Yet *The Death of the Hat: A Brief History of Poetry in 50 Objects* was particularly challenging. First, early poets, particularly in the West, composed philosophical and spiritual meditations on life and death, and only rarely wrote about *objects*. Finding early poems written by women was another challenge. Certainly women wrote poems in earlier eras — Jusammi Chikako, Phillis Wheatley, and Charlotte Smith among them — but, at least in the West, poetry written by men was more likely to find its way into print.

Any short introduction must be general. Such is the case with this one. The important thing to remember about literary eras and ages, with all their dates and characteristics, is that little of it can ever be precise. The writers of one era may exhibit some of the qualities of an earlier era. Poets of one age continue to write into the next. And the literary ages defined here are largely Western; poetry in other parts of the world underwent somewhat different evolutions. Nonetheless, I could not ignore the strong poems I found from Eastern poets. I've included a taste of these, though this collection does not do them justice.

The major literary periods that I've used as an organizing principle are the ones about which most literary historians agree. Within these major eras were small eras and movements, like the Elizabethan Age during the Renaissance. The Elizabethan Age begins with the coronation of Queen Elizabeth I and ends with her death forty-five years later. However, that's not to say that when Elizabeth died, word went out far and wide in England that poets were to no longer write "Elizabethan poetry." Rather, the change was gradual.

The early Middle Ages, sometimes called the Dark Ages (400–1000), were brutal, barbaric, and cruel. When the Roman Empire fell, in 410, the stability that most of Europe had experienced crumbled. Battles raged across the land. The Black Plague, caused by a bacteria spread by rats, swept Europe, killing nearly two-thirds of the population. Creating enduring works of literature and art was not a priority for the people of this era. One of the

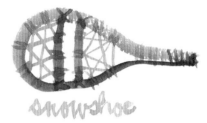
snowshoe

few lasting pieces of literature created during this time was *Beowulf,* an epic poem written by a long-forgotten Anglo-Saxon. Set in Scandinavia, the poem describes the rampage of Grendel, a beast that threatened the countryside.

Of course, the warfare of the Dark Ages did not end overnight. The High Middle Ages, which lasted five hundred years (1000–1500), were a time when the more powerful European lords vanquished their weaker neighbors, leading to city-states that eventually became Italy, Germany, and England. Following the Norman conquest of England in 1066, literature became a more important part of the culture. Ballads, romantic stories of the knights, and allegorical poems began to appear. There were a few large cities — such as Paris, Venice, Florence, and Milan — that became centers of learning and culture. In these cities, particularly Florence, grew the seeds that would become the Renaissance.

A number of literary masterpieces were created during the High Middle Ages in various places in the world. The poet Rumi lived and worked in thirteenth-century Persia. Dante Alighieri wrote his masterpiece, *The Divine Comedy,* in early fourteenth-century Italy. In late fourteenth-century England, Geoffrey Chaucer wrote a series of stories called *The Canterbury Tales*.

During the Renaissance (1500–late 1600s), Europe came alive with literature, science, and art. While there's no exact starting date or place for this period of history that changed the world, Florence, Italy, is generally accepted as its birthplace. One of the key influences of the period was the spreading innovation of movable type, which allowed for the inexpensive printing of works of literature. Suddenly, books were available to the masses, not just to the Catholic Church and well-heeled landowners. All manner of literature appeared. The Renaissance was, of course, the age of Shakespeare and Michelangelo. It was the age of the sonnet and elegy, lyric poems and pastoral poems, often recited to the accompaniment of music.

Like all cultural movements, the Renaissance did not last forever. The optimism of the age and the era's cultural advances made some people uncomfortable, especially those in the Church. It was time, they believed, to focus on reason and political progress. The new era, the Enlightenment, or Age of

11

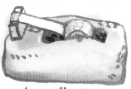
tape dispenser

Reason (late 1600s–1785), would follow the path of rationality (head over heart, if you will) as a way of finding a universal system of beliefs. It was to be a time of reasoned behavior, conversations, and ideas. Consequently, it was not an age known for its poetry, other than the work of Alexander Pope, who offered book-length poems, including *An Essay on Man* and *An Essay on Criticism*.

Toward the end of the eighteenth century, the cultural pendulum swung again for a short but luminous time — the Romantic Period. This era lasted less than fifty years (1785–1830) and was largely built on the work of seven poets — among them, John Keats, Lord Byron, and Percy Bysshe Shelley — most of whom died at an early age. Reacting against the confines and formalism of the Enlightenment, poets of the Romantic Period were spontaneous, imaginative, and emotional. They reveled in a connection to nature. In fact, nature became central to their work. The highbrow, formal language of the Enlightenment was replaced by a more natural vocabulary and rhythm. Rigid rhymed stanzas were replaced by less structured blank verse.

Although this period is usually said to end in 1830, around the start of the Victorian era, many poets of the Victorian Period — such as Edgar Allan Poe, Walt Whitman, and Henry Wadsworth Longfellow — wrote like those of the Romantic Period.

The Victorian era was the age of the steam engine, industrialization, urbanization. It was a time of change and upheaval in England and Europe. So, too, it was the age of overcrowding in the cities, poverty, and child-labor abuses. Despite the enormous popularity of Charles Dickens, poetry remained the prominent genre, with many poets writing realistic poetry, often on social topics, such as Elizabeth Barrett Browning's "The Cry of the Children," a long poem that laments the dangers of child labor.

The Modern Period began at the end of the nineteenth century. If it had a battle cry, it was poet Ezra Pound's declaration to "Make it new." It was an age of experimentation in rhythm, language, form, and theme, all of which can be found in "The Waste Land," a long poem by T. S. Eliot. Artists in all fields were reevaluating and reinventing their art forms. And poets were no exception. Artists questioned

Sweetgum leaf

"self," asking where and how they belonged in a world that was on the brink of war, when many people were feeling alienated and fragmented. Poets reacted to the sprawl of urban areas, increased population, and to the changes in transportation and architecture. The cutting-edge poets — including Marianne Moore, e. e. cummings, and William Carlos Williams — turned their backs on the realism of the Victorian writers, concentrating instead on the images in their poems. The Harlem Renaissance, which saw a rebirth in the popularity of African-American writing and art, lasted through the 1920s. The Modern Period ended with the so-called confessional poets, such as Robert Lowell and Sylvia Plath, of the Postmodern Period.

If the poets of the modern era wanted to "make it new," the postmodern poets questioned what "it" really was. They wrote poetry that was more free form than the poems of any of their predecessors. The postmodern poetic style was meant to reflect the way people spoke and thought, what is called "stream of consciousness." As a result, much poetry of the Postmodern Period seems disjointed, even random at times. In a world that seemed even more

chaotic than the world of the first few decades of the twentieth century, these poets wrote of the meaninglessness of the reality that they saw swirling around them. Their poems reflect the turmoil of the world with their shapelessness, lack of structure, and random line breaks, making postmodern poems often difficult to understand at first reading. Among the most recognized of these poets are the Beat poets, including Allen Ginsberg, Lawrence Ferlinghetti, and Anne Waldman.

I hope that *The Death of the Hat: A Brief History of Poetry in 50 Objects* gives you a better idea of how poetry has evolved. I hope, too, that you enjoy a handful of the poets enough that you decide to explore their work further. Perhaps you will read more poets of the Harlem Renaissance or poems by Christina Rossetti. Finally, I believe that poetry is meant to be shared — that's what anthologies are all about — so I hope you share a couple of these poems with someone close to you.

moon snail

Things

Eloise Greenfield

Went to the corner

Walked in the store

Bought me some candy

Ain't got it no more

Ain't got it no more

Went to the beach

Played on the shore

Built me a sandhouse

Ain't got it no more

Ain't got it no more

Went to the kitchen

Lay down on the floor

Made me a poem

Still got it

Still got it

A Bookworm

Anonymous
translated by Craig Williamson

A moth ate a word.   To me that seemed
A curious happening   when I heard of that wonder,
That a worm should swallow   the word of a man,
A thief in the dark   eat a thoughtful discourse
And the strong base it stood on.   He stole, but he was not
A whit the wiser   when the word had been swallowed.

A Solitary Wildgoose

Cui Tu
translated by Witter Bynner

Line after line has flown back over the border.

Where are you headed all by yourself?

In the evening rain you call to them —

And slowly you alight on an icy pond.

The low wet clouds move faster than you

Along the wall toward the cold moon.

. . . If they caught you in a net or with a shot,

Would it be worse than flying alone?

17

Grass

Bai Juyi
translated by Lan Hua

Far far across the plain

Spreads the grass

One year to another

It withers and returns

Never extinguished

By the prairie fires

With Spring wind

It leaps back to life

Bringing near a fragrance

From an age-old path

As the green sward overgrows

Crumbling city walls

So once again my friend

We must part

With feelings deep as grass

Overtaking my heart

In Praise of a Sword Given Him by His Prince

Colman mac Lenini
translated by Richard O'Connell

Blackbirds to a swan,

Feathers to hard iron,

Rock hags to a siren,

    All lords to my lord;

Jackdaws to a hawk,

Cackling to a choir,

Sparks to a bonfire,

    All swords to my sword.

Grainfield

Ibn 'Iyād
translated by Cole Frazen

Look at the ripe wheat

bending before the wind

like squadrons of horsemen

fleeing in defeat, bleeding

from the wounds of the poppies.

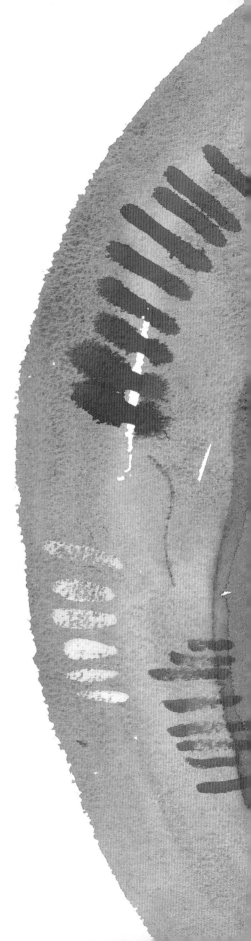

A Just-Finishing Candle

Rumi
translated by Coleman Barks

A candle is made to become entirely flame.
In that annihilating moment
it has no shadow.

It is nothing but a tongue of light
describing a refuge.

Look at this
just-finishing candle stub
as someone who is finally safe
from virtue and vice,

the pride and the shame
we claim from those.

Jusammi Chikako
translated by Edwin A. Cranston

On this summer night
All the household lies asleep,
And in the doorway,
For once open after dark,
Stands the moon, brilliant, cloudless.

Bashō
translated by Robert Hass

Midnight frost—

I'd borrow

the scarecrow's shirt.

25

from Mercutio's Queen Mab Speech

William Shakespeare

O, then I see Queen Mab hath been with you.

She is the fairies' midwife, and she comes

In shape no bigger than an agate stone

On the forefinger of an alderman,

Drawn with a team of little atomi

Over men's noses as they lie asleep.

Her wagon spokes made of long spinners' legs

The cover of the wings of grasshoppers,

Her traces of the smallest spider web,

Her collars of the moonshine's wat'ry beams,

Her whip of cricket's bone, the lash of film,

Her wagoner a small gray-coated gnat,

Not half so big as a round little worm

Pricked from the lazy finger of a maid.

Her chariot is an empty hazelnut,

Made by the joiner squirrel or old grub,

Time out o' mind the fairies' coachmakers.

So Breaks the Sun

Ben Jonson

So breaks the sun earth's **rugged** chains
   Wherein rude winter bound her veins,
So grows both stream and source of price
   That lately fettered were with ice,
So naked trees get crisped heads,
   And colored coats the roughest meads,
And all get vigor, youth, and sprite,
   That are but looked on by his light.

A Burnt Ship

John Donne

Out of a fired ship, which by no way

But drowning could be rescued from the flame,

Some men leap'd forth, and ever as they came

Near the foes' ships, did by their shot decay;

So all were lost, which in the ship were found,

They in the sea being burnt, they in the burnt ship drown'd.

29

Stick and Hat

Emperor Lê Thánh Tông
translated by John S. Major

They're insignificant when not in use,

But work wonders when properly employed.

In times of peril, sticks strong and true defend the realm;

Whatever the weather, all take shelter beneath their wide-woven hats.

The stick preserves the peace and plenty of the land,

The hat gives shade and refuge to the world.

What marvels they make possible, when used this way:

The hand wields power, as the head directs and leads.

Kim Ku
translated by Kevin O'Rourke

I spy the three-colored peach blossom

floating down the mountain stream.

A free spirit, I jump in, fully clothed.

Flowers scooped

in my arms, I splash up and down in the water.

An Hymn to the Evening

Phillis Wheatley

Soon as the sun forsook the eastern main

The pealing thunder shook the heav'nly plain;

Majestic grandeur! From the zephyr's wings,

Exhales the incense of the blooming spring.

Soft purl the streams, the birds renew their notes,

And through the air their mingled music floats.

    Through all the heav'ns what beauteous dies are spread!

But the west glories in the deepest red:

So may our breasts with ev'ry virtue glow,

The living temples of our God below!

Fill'd with the praise of him who gives the light,

And draws the sable curtains of the night,

Let placid slumbers sooth each weary mind,

At morn to wake more heav'nly, more refin'd,

So shall the labours of the day begin

More pure, more guarded from the snares of sin.

Night's leaden scepter seals my drowsy eyes,

Then cease, my song, till fair *Aurora* rise.

Retort on Mordaunt's "The Call"

John Scott of Amwell

I hate that drum's discordant sound,
Parading round, and round, and round:
To thoughtless youth it pleasure yields,
And lures from cities and from fields,
To sell their liberty for charms
Of tawdry lace, and glittering arms;
And when Ambition's voice commands,
To march, and fight, and fall, in foreign lands.

I hate that drum's discordant sound,
Parading round, and round, and round;
To me it talks of ravag'd plains,
And burning towns, and ruin'd swains,
And mangled limbs, and dying groans,
And widows' tears, and orphans' moans;
And all that Misery's hand bestows,
To fill the catalogue of human woes.

A Red, Red Rose

Robert Burns

O my Luve is like a red, red rose
    That's newly sprung in June;
O my Luve is like the melody
    That's sweetly played in tune.

So fair art thou, my bonnie lass,
    So deep in luve am I;
And I will luve thee still, my dear,
    Till a' the seas gang dry.

Till a' the seas gang dry, my dear,
    And the rocks melt wi' the sun;
I will love thee still, my dear,
    While the sands o' life shall run.

And fare thee weel, my only luve!
    And fare thee weel awhile!
And I will come again, my luve,
    Though it were ten thousand mile.

The Sick Rose

William Blake

O Rose, thou art sick —
The invisible worm,
That flies in the night
In the howling storm,

Has found out thy bed
Of crimson joy;
And his dark secret love
Does thy life destroy.

To the moon

Charlotte Smith

Queen of the silver bow! — by the pale beam,
   Alone and pensive, I delight to stray,
And watch thy shadow trembling in the stream,
   Or mark the floating clouds that cross thy way.
And while I gaze, thy mild and placid light
   Sheds a soft calm upon my troubled breast;
And oft I think — fair planet of the night,
   That in thy orb, the wretched may have rest:
The sufferers of the earth perhaps may go,
   Released by death — to thy benignant sphere,
And the sad children of Despair and Woe
   Forget, in thee, their cup of sorrow here.
Oh! that I soon may reach thy world serene,
   Poor wearied pilgrim — in this toiling scene!

A Riddle, On the Letter E

George Gordon, Lord Byron

The beginning of eternity, the end of time and space,

The beginning of every end, and the end of every place.

Mouse's Nest

John Clare

I found a ball of grass among the hay

And progged it as I passed and went away;

And when I looked I fancied something stirred,

And turned agen and hoped to catch the bird —

When out an old mouse bolted in the wheats

With all her young ones hanging at her teats;

She looked so odd and so grotesque to me,

I ran and wondered what the thing could be,

And pushed the knapweed bunches where I stood;

Then the mouse hurried from the craking brood.

The young ones squeaked, and as I went away

She found her nest again among the hay.

The water o'er the pebbles scarce could run

And broad old cesspools glittered in the sun.

I Wandered Lonely as a Cloud

William Wordsworth

I wandered lonely as a cloud
That floats on high o'er vales and hills,
When all at once I saw a crowd,
A host, of golden daffodils;
Beside the lake, beneath the trees,
Fluttering and dancing in the breeze.

Continuous as the stars that shine
And twinkle on the milky way,
They stretched in never-ending line
Along the margin of a bay:
Ten thousand saw I at a glance,
Tossing their heads in sprightly dance.

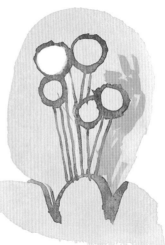

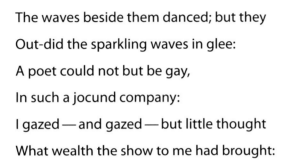

The waves beside them danced; but they

Out-did the sparkling waves in glee:

A poet could not but be gay,

In such a jocund company:

I gazed — and gazed — but little thought

What wealth the show to me had brought:

For oft, when on my couch I lie

In vacant or in pensive mood,

They flash upon that inward eye

Which is the bliss of solitude;

And then my heart with pleasure fills,

And dances with the daffodils.

The Eagle

Alfred, Lord Tennyson

He clasps the crag with crooked hands;
Close to the sun in lonely lands,
Ring'd with the azure world, he stands.

The wrinkled sea beneath him crawls;
He watches from his mountain walls,
And like a thunderbolt he falls.

Snow-Flakes

Henry Wadsworth Longfellow

Out of the bosom of the Air,
    Out of the cloud-folds of her garments shaken,
Over the woodlands brown and bare
    Over the harvest-fields forsaken,
        Silent, and soft, and slow
        Descends the snow.

Even as our cloudy fancies take
    Suddenly shape in some divine expression,
Even as the troubled heart doth make
    In the white countenance confession,
        The troubled sky reveals
        The grief it feels.

This is the poem of the air,
    Slowly in silent syllables recorded;
This is the secret of despair,
    Long in its cloudy bosom hoarded,
        Now whispered and revealed
        To wood and field.

The Haunted Palace

Edgar Allan Poe

In the greenest of our valleys
    By good angels tenanted,
Once a fair and stately palace —
    Radiant palace — reared its head.
In the monarch Thought's dominion —
    It stood there!
Never seraph spread a pinion
    Over fabric half so fair!

Banners yellow, glorious, golden,
    On its roof did float and flow
(This — all this — was in the olden
    Time long ago,)
And every gentle air that dallied,
    In that sweet day,
Along the ramparts plumed and pallid,
    A wingéd odour went away.

Wanderers in that happy valley,
    Through two luminous windows, saw
Spirits moving musically
    To a lute's well-tunéd law,
Round about a throne where, sitting
    (Porphyrogene!)
In state his glory well befitting,
    The ruler of the realm was seen.

And all with pearl and ruby glowing
　　Was the fair palace door,
Through which came flowing, flowing, flowing
　　And sparkling evermore,
A troop of Echoes, whose sweet duty
　　Was but to sing,
In voices of surpassing beauty,
　　The wit and wisdom of their king.

But evil things, in robes of sorrow,
　　Assailed the monarch's high estate.
(Ah, let us mourn! — for never morrow
　　Shall dawn upon him desolate!)
And round about his home the glory
　　That blushed and bloomed,
Is but a dim-remembered story
　　Of the old time entombed.

And travellers, now, within that valley,
　　Through the red-litten windows see
Vast forms, that move fantastically
　　To a discordant melody,
While, like a ghastly rapid river,
　　Through the pale door
A hideous throng rush out forever
　　And laugh — but smile no more.

45

The Dismantled Ship

Walt Whitman

In some unused lagoon, some nameless bay,

On sluggish, lonesome waters, anchor'd near the shore,

An old, dismasted, gray and batter'd ship, disabled, done,

After free voyages to all the seas of earth, haul'd up at last and hawser'd tight,

Lies rusting, mouldering.

Street Lanterns

Mary Elizabeth Coleridge

Country roads are yellow and brown.
We mend the roads in London town.

Never a hansom dare come nigh.
Never a cart goes rolling by,

An unwonted silence steals
In between the turning wheels.

Quickly ends the autumn day,
And the workman goes his way,

Leaving, midst the traffic rude,
One small isle of solitude,

Lit, throughout the lengthy night,
By the little lantern's light.

Jewels of the dark have we,
Brighter than the rustic's be.

Over the dull earth are thrown
Topaz, and the ruby stone.

My Shadow

Robert Louis Stevenson

I have a little shadow that goes in and out with me,

And what can be the use of him is more than I can see.

He is very, very like me from the heels up to the head;

And I see him jump before me, when I jump into my bed.

The funniest thing about him is the way he likes to grow —

Not at all like proper children, which is always very slow;

For he sometimes shoots up taller like an india-rubber ball,

And he sometimes gets so little that there's none of him at all.

He hasn't got a notion of how children ought to play,

And can only make a fool of me in every sort of way.

He stays so close beside me, he's a coward you can see;

I'd think shame to stick to nursie as that shadow sticks to me!

One morning, very early, before the sun was up,

I rose and found the shining dew on every buttercup;

But my lazy little shadow, like an arrant sleepy-head,

Had stayed at home behind me and was fast asleep in bed.

Cobwebs

Christina Georgina Rossetti

It is a land with neither night nor day,
    Nor heat nor cold, nor any wind nor rain,
    Nor hills nor valleys: but one even plain
Stretches through long unbroken miles away,
While through the sluggish air a twilight grey
    Broodeth: no moons or seasons wax and wane,
    No ebb and flow are there along the main,
No bud-time, no leaf-falling, there for aye:—
No ripple on the sea, no shifting sand,
    No beat of wings to stir the stagnant space:
No pulse of life through all the loveless land
And loveless sea; no trace of days before,
    No guarded home, no toil-won resting-place,
No future hope, no fear for evermore.

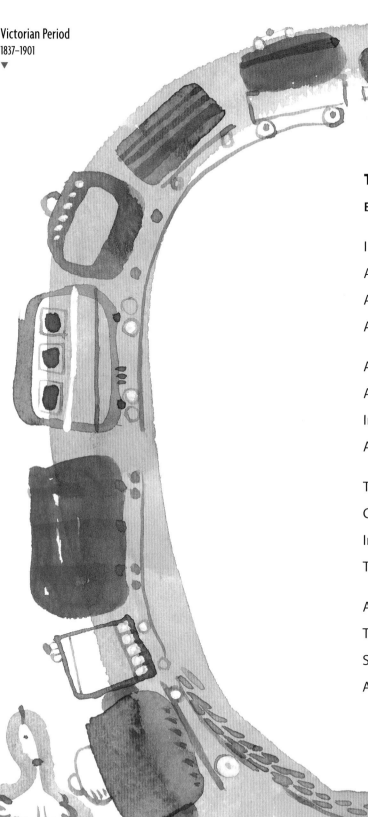

The Railway Train

Emily Dickinson

I like to see it lap the miles,
And lick the valleys up,
And stop to feed itself at tanks;
And then, prodigious, step

Around a pile of mountains,
And, supercilious, peer
In shanties by the sides of roads;
And then a quarry pare

To fit its sides, and crawl between,
Complaining all the while
In horrid, hooting stanza;
Then chase itself down hill

And neigh like Boanerges;
Then, punctual as a star,
Stop — docile and omnipotent —
At its own stable door.

The Red Wheelbarrow

William Carlos Williams

so much depends

upon

a red wheel

barrow

glazed with rain

water

beside the white

chickens

51

The Love Tree

Countee Cullen

Come, let us plant our love as farmers plant

A seed, and you shall water it with tears,

And I shall weed it with my hands until

They bleed. Perchance this buried love of ours

Will fall on goodly ground and bear a tree

With fruit and flowers; pale lovers chancing here

May pluck and eat, and through their veins a sweet

And languid ardor play, their pulses beat

An unimagined tune, their shy lips meet

And part, and bliss repeat again. And men

Will pilgrimage from far and wide to see

This tree for which we two were crucified,

And, happy in themselves, will never know

'Twas break of heart that made the Love Tree grow.

Fan-Piece for Her Imperial Lord

Ezra Pound

O fan of white silk,
    clear as frost on the grass-blade,
You also are laid aside.

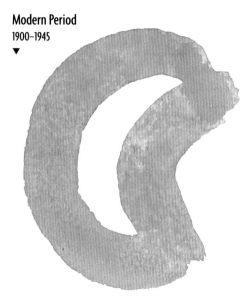

The Cat and the Moon

William Butler Yeats

The cat went here and there

And the moon spun round like a top,

And the nearest kin of the moon

The creeping cat looked up.

Black Minnaloushe stared at the moon,

For wander and wail as he would

The pure cold light in the sky

Troubled his animal blood.

Minnaloushe runs in the grass,

Lifting his delicate feet.

Do you dance, Minnaloushe, do you dance?

When two close kindred meet

What better than call a dance,

Maybe the moon may learn,

Tired of that courtly fashion,

A new dance turn.

Minnaloushe creeps through the grass

From moonlit place to place,

The sacred moon overhead

Has taken a new phase.

Does Minnaloushe know that his pupils

Will pass from change to change,

And that from round to crescent,

From crescent to round they range?

Minnaloushe creeps through the grass

Alone, important and wise,

And lifts to the changing moon

His changing eyes.

Stars

Langston Hughes

O, sweep of stars over Harlem streets,

O, little breath of oblivion that is night.

    A city building

       To a mother's song.

    A city dreaming

       To a lullaby.

Reach up your hand, dark boy, and take a star.

Out of the little breath of oblivion

       That is night,

       Take just

       One star.

A Cloud Shadow

Robert Frost

A breeze discovered my open book
And began to flutter the leaves to look
For a poem there used to be on Spring.
I tried to tell her "There's no such thing!"

For whom would a poem on Spring be by?
The breeze disdained to make reply;
And a cloud shadow crossed her face
For fear I would make her miss the place.

57

Driftwood

Witter Bynner

Come, warm your hands
From the cold wind of time.
I have built here, under the moon
A many-colored fire
With fragments of wood
That have been part of a tree
And part of a ship.

Were leaves more real,
Or driven nails,
Or fingers of builders,
Than these burning violets?
Come, warm your hands
From the cold wind of time
There's a fire under the moon.

Boxes and Bags

Carl Sandburg

The bigger the box the more it holds.

Empty boxes hold the same as empty heads.

Enough small empty boxes thrown into a big empty box fill it full.

A half-empty box says, "Put more in."

A big enough box could hold the world.

Elephants need big boxes to hold a dozen elephant handkerchiefs.

Fleas fold little handkerchiefs and fix them nice and neat in flea handker-
chief-boxes.

Bags lean against each other and boxes stand independent.

Boxes are square with corners unless round with circles.

Box can be piled on box till the whole works comes tumbling.

Pile box on box and the bottom box says, "If you will kindly take notice
you will see it all rests on me."

Pile box on box and the top one says, "Who falls farthest if or when we
fall? I ask you."

Box people go looking for boxes and bag people go looking for bags.

City Trees

Edna St. Vincent Millay

The trees along this city street,
    Save for the traffic and the trains,
Would make a sound as thin and sweet
    As trees in country lanes.

And people standing in their shade
    Out of a shower, undoubtedly
Would hear such music as is made
    Upon a country tree.

Oh, little leaves that are so dumb
    Against the shrieking city air,
I watch you when the wind has come, —
    I know what sound is there.

Manhole Covers

Karl Shapiro

The beauty of manhole covers — what of that?

Like medals struck by a great savage khan,

Like Mayan calendar stones, unliftable, indecipherable,

Not like the old electrum, chased and scored,

Mottoed and sculptured to a turn,

But notched and whelked and pocked and smashed

With the great company names

(Gentle Bethlehem, smiling United States).

This rustproof artifact of my street,

Long after roads are melted away will lie

Sidewise in the grave of the iron-old world,

Bitten at the edges,

Strong with its cryptic American,

Its dated beauty.

Mushrooms

Sylvia Plath

Overnight, very
Whitely, discreetly,
Very quietly

Our toes, our noses
Take hold on the loam,
Acquire the air.

Nobody sees us,
Stops us, betrays us;
The small grains make room.

Soft fists insist on
Heaving the needles,
The leafy bedding,

Even the paving.
Our hammers, our rams,
Earless and eyeless,

Perfectly voiceless,
Widen the crannies,
Shoulder through holes. We

Diet on water,
On crumbs of shadow,
Bland-mannered, asking

Little or nothing.
So many of us!
So many of us!

We are shelves, we are
Tables, we are meek,
We are edible,

Nudgers and shovers
In spite of ourselves.
Our kind multiplies:

We shall by morning
Inherit the earth.
Our foot's in the door.

63

Lament, for Cocoa

John Updike

The scum has come.
   My cocoa's cold.
The cup is numb,
   And I grow old.

It seems an age
   Since from the pot
It bubbled, beige
   And burning hot —

Too hot to be
   Too quickly quaffed.
Accordingly,
   I found a draft

And in it placed
   The boiling brew
And took a taste
   Of toast or two.

Alas, time flies
   And minutes chill;
My cocoa lies
   Dull brown and still.

How wearisome!
   In likelihood,
The scum, once come,
   Is come for good.

e. e. cummings

i thank You God for most this amazing

day:for the leaping greenly spirits of trees

and a blue true dream of sky;and for everything

which is natural which is infinite which is yes

(i who have died am alive again today,

and this is the sun's birthday;this is the birth

day of life and of love and wings:and of the gay

great happening illimitably earth)

how should tasting touching hearing seeing

breathing any — lifted from the no

of all nothing — human merely being

doubt unimaginable You?

(now the ears of my ears awake and

now the eyes of my eyes are opened)

65

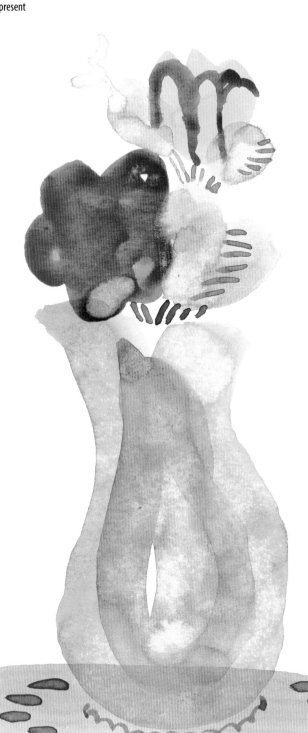

The Cat

Lawrence Ferlinghetti

The cat

licks its paw and

lies down in

the bookshelf nook

She

can lie in a

sphinx position

without moving for so

many hours

and then turn her head

to me and

rise and stretch

and turn

her back to me and

lick her paw again as if

no real time had passed

It hasn't

and she is the sphinx with

all the time in the world

in the desert of her time

The cat

    knows where flies die

        sees ghosts in motes of air

            and shadows in sunbeams

She hears

    the music of the spheres and

the hum in the wires of houses

    and the hum of the universe

in interstellar spaces

        but

prefers domestic places

    and the hum of the heater

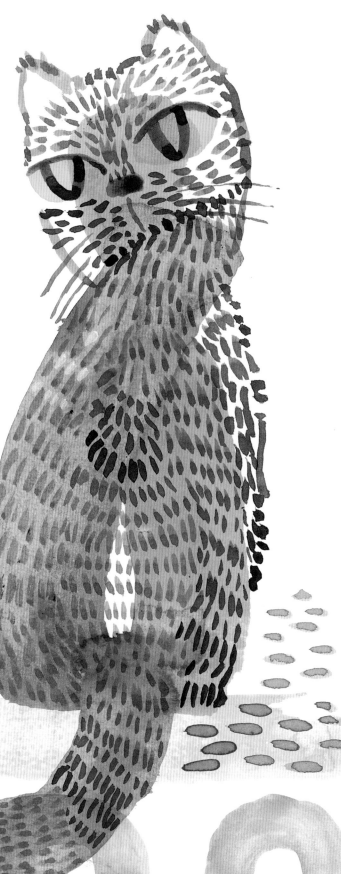

Ode to a Stamp Album

Pablo Neruda

Album of perfect stamps!

Butterflies,

ships,

sea shapes, corollas,

leaning towers,

dark eyes, moist and

round as grapes,

album

smooth

as

a

slippery

fish,

with thousands

of glistening

scales,

each page

a

racing

charger

in search of

distant pleasures, forgotten

flowers!

Other pages are

bonfires or carnations,

red clusters of stones

set afire

by a secret ruby,

some display

the snow,

the doves

of Norway,

the architectural clarity of the dew.

How was it possible

to bring

to paper

such beauty,

so many

expeditions

into infinity?

How

possible

to capture

the ineffable

glow

of

the Sambuca

butterfly

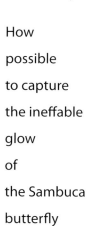

and its phosphorescent

caterpillar colonies,

and,

as well,

that

gentle

locomotive

puffing through pastures

like an

iron

bull,

small

but fiery,

and that

fauna from a distant sun,

elegant

wasps,

sea serpents,

incredible

camels?

World of miracles!

Insatiable

spiral,

comet's tail

of all earth's

highways,

dictionary

of the wind,

star-struck album

bulging

with noble

fruits and territories,

treasure-keeper

sailing

on its treasure,

garnet

pomegranate,

nomadic

stamp album!

The Summer Day

Mary Oliver

Who made the world?

Who made the swan, and the black bear?

Who made the grasshopper?

This grasshopper, I mean —

the one who has flung herself out of the grass,

the one who is eating sugar out of my hand,

who is moving her jaws back and forth instead of up and down —

who is gazing around with her enormous and complicated eyes.

Now she lifts her pale forearms and thoroughly washes her face.

Now she snaps her wings open, and floats away.

I don't know exactly what a prayer is.

I do know how to pay attention, how to fall down

into the grass, how to kneel down in the grass,

how to be idle and blessed, how to stroll through the fields,

which is what I have been doing all day.

Tell me, what else should I have done?

Doesn't everything die at last, and too soon?

Tell me, what is it you plan to do

with your one wild and precious life?

A Birthday Card

Ted Kooser

In her eighties now, and weak and ill
with emphysema, my aunt sends me
a birthday card — a tossing ocean
with clipper ship — and wishes me well
at forty-four. She's included
a note — hard-bitten in ballpoint,
with a pen that sometimes skips whole words
but never turns back — to tell me
her end of the news: how the steroids
have softened her spine, how
every X ray shows more shattered bone.
Her hasty words skip in and out,
their little grooves washed clean of ink,
the message rising and falling
like short-wave radio, sending
this hurried S.O.S., with love.

The Death of the Hat

Billy Collins

Once every man wore a hat.

In the ashen newsreels,
the avenues of cities
are broad rivers flowing with hats.

The ballparks swelled
with thousands of strawhats,
brims and bands,
rows of men smoking
and cheering in shirtsleeves.

Hats were the law.
They went without saying.
You noticed a man without a hat in a crowd.

You bought them from Adams or Dobbs
who branded your initials in gold
on the inside band.

Trolleys crisscrossed the city.
Steamships sailed in and out of the harbor.
Men with hats gathered on the docks.

There was a person to block your hat
and a hatcheck girl to mind it
while you had a drink
or ate a steak with peas and a baked potato.
In your office stood a hat rack.

The day war was declared
everyone in the street was wearing a hat.
And they were wearing hats
when a ship loaded with men sank in the icy sea.

My father wore one to work every day
and returned home
carrying the evening paper,
the winter chill radiating from his overcoat.

But today we go bareheaded
into the winter streets,
stand hatless on frozen platforms.

Today the mailboxes on the roadside
and the spruce trees behind the house
wear cold white hats of snow.

Mice scurry from the stone walls at night
in their thin fur hats
to eat the birdseed that has spilled.

And now my father, after a life of work,
wears a hat of earth,
and on top of that,
a lighter one of cloud and sky — a hat of wind.

Flash Cards

Rita Dove

In math I was the whiz kid, keeper
of oranges and apples. *What you don't understand,
master,* my father said; the faster
I answered, the faster they came.

I could see one bud on the teacher's geranium,
one clear bee sputtering at the wet pane.
The tulip trees always dragged after heavy rain
so I tucked my head as my boots slapped home.

My father put up his feet after work
and relaxed with a highball and *The Life of Lincoln.*
After supper we drilled and I climbed the dark

before sleep, before a thin voice hissed
numbers as I spun on a wheel. I had to guess.
Ten, I kept saying, *I'm only ten.*

Famous

Naomi Shihab Nye

The river is famous to the fish.

The loud voice is famous to silence,
which knew it would inherit the earth
before anybody said so.

The cat sleeping on the fence is famous to the birds
watching him from the birdhouse.

The tear is famous, briefly, to the cheek.

The idea you carry close to your bosom
is famous to your bosom.

The boot is famous to the earth,
more famous than the dress shoe,
which is famous only to floors.

The bent photograph is famous to the one who carries it
and not at all famous to the one who is pictured.

I want to be famous to shuffling men
who smile while crossing streets,
sticky children in grocery lines,
famous as the one who smiled back.

I want to be famous in the way a pulley is famous,
or a buttonhole, not because it did anything spectacular,
but because it never forgot what it could do.

Acknowledgments

"Things" by Eloise Greenfield. Text copyright © 1978 by Eloise Greenfield. Used by permission of HarperCollins Publishers.

"A Bookworm" from *A Feast of Creatures: Anglo-Saxon Riddle-Songs,* edited and translated by Craig Williamson. Copyright © 1982 University of Pennsylvania Press. Reprinted with permission of the University of Pennsylvania Press.

"A Solitary Wildgoose" by Cui Tu, translated by Witter Bynner. From *Three Hundred Poems of the T'ang Dynasty*. Reprinted by permission of the Witter Bynner Foundation for Poetry.

"Grass" by Bai Juyi, translated by Lan Hua. Reprinted by permission of Epoch Times.

"Grainfield" by Ibn 'Iyād. Translation copyright © 1989 by Cole Franzen. Reprinted by permission of City Lights Books.

"A Just-Finishing Candle" by Rumi, translated by Coleman Barks. Reprinted by permission of Coleman Barks.

Haiku by Bashō [p. 30: "Midnight frost"] from *The Essential Haiku: Versions of Bashō, Buson & Issa,* edited with an introduction by Robert Hass. Introduction and selection copyright © 1994 by Robert Hass. Unless otherwise noted, all translations copyright © 1994 by Robert Hass. Reprinted by permission of HarperCollins Publishers.

"Stick and Hat" by Emperor Lê Thánh Tông, translated by John S. Major. Courtesy of John S. Major.

"I spy the three-colored peach blossom" by Kim Ku. Reprinted with permission from *The Book of Korean Shijo,* translated and edited by Kevin O'Rourke, Harvard East Asian Monographs 215, Harvard University Asia Center, Cambridge, Massachusetts, 2002, p. 49. © 2002 by the President and Fellows of Harvard College. Further reproduction or distribution of this material is prohibited.

"The Red Wheelbarrow" by William Carlos Williams, from *The Collected Poems: Volume 1: 1909–1939,* copyright 1938 by New Directions Publishing Corp. Reprinted by permission of New Directions Publishing Corp.

"The Love Tree" by Countee Cullen. From *Copper Sun,* copyright 1927 Harper & Bros., NY, renewed 1954 by Ida M. Cullen. Copyrights held by Amistad Research Center, Tulane University. Administered by Thompson and Thompson, Brooklyn, NY.

"Stars" from *The Collected Poems of Langston Hughes* by Langston Hughes, edited by Arnold Rampersad with David Roessel, Associate Editor, copyright © 1994 by the Estate of Langston Hughes. Used by permission of Alfred A. Knopf, an imprint of the Knopf Doubleday Publishing Group, a division of Random House LLC. All rights reserved.

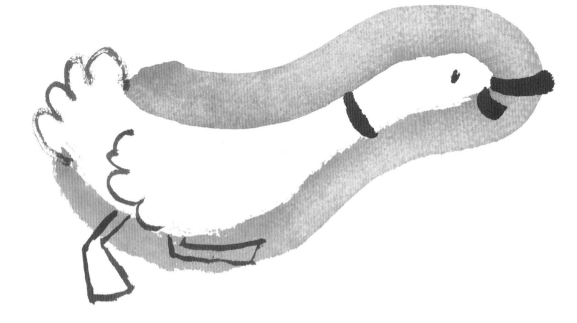